THE WINTER GARDEN

PENHALIGON'S SCENTED TREASURY
OF WINTER VERSE AND PROSE

For A.A.W.

⸂THE⸃
WINTER GARDEN

EDITED BY
SHEILA PICKLES

LONDON MCMXCII

INTRODUCTION

Dear Reader,

It is said that whenever the English meet, the first thing they talk about is the weather. Never is it more apparent than in the passages I have selected for The Winter Garden, the fourth in my series of seasonal treasuries. Perhaps because it was cold outside and conditions were grim, keeping warm was always at the forefront of the writers' minds; but the wintry beauty of the landscape did not elude them and some of our most lyrical poetry was written about this chilling season.

However much the birds and farmers despised the snowy weather, it was always welcomed by the children. For only when the snow lay thick on the ground and the ice firm on the lake could they toboggan and skate. These wintry pastimes play a large part in the pastoral calendar and are finely observed by all our great classical writers from Jane Austen to Charles Dickens.

Winter is also the season of tradition. For generations the Christmas pantomime or ballet has been the English child's introduction to the theatre. Houses are dressed with holly and trees with ornaments and lights, just as George Eliot describes in *The Mill on the Floss.* The church calendar is observed, carols are sung and Christmas fayre enjoyed by all. The continuity of the old traditions brings reassurance at a time of unrest and I hope that this small book will bring you comfort and joy.

Sheila Pickles, London, Christmas 1992

POT-POURRI

ONCE the frost comes and snow lies on the ground, the garden is a poor source of material for pot-pourri. Fir cones and dried flowers may be gathered earlier in the year but I like to mix in other spicy ingredients and nuts to give a seasonal feel. Indian food shops are a rich hunting ground for dried spices and seeds but these should be introduced in small quantities for their scent is strong. The larder may also provide ideas – whole nutmegs may be included, along with cinnamon sticks, cloves and matchsticks of orange peel. There are many possibilities for a winter bowl, and anything you cannot find at home may be obtained from a good herbalist. I place importance on the mix looking rich and handsome and being quite dry and then I add a good spicy oil.

Depending on where the pot-pourri is to be used, additional garnishes may be added. I like to put our Winter Garden pot-pourri into large dark wooden bowls which add an atmospheric note to a gentleman's dressing room or study. With nuts and orange peel on top they add a festive air to a dining-room table.

Pot-pourri is one of the few really effective ways to change the atmosphere of a room from season to season. Top it with ribbon, or put it in a pretty china bowl. With simple touches, your own pot-pourri will give you hours of pleasure during the darkest months of the year.

WINTER-TIME

LATE lies the wintry sun a-bed,
A frosty, fiery sleepy-head;
Blinks but an hour or two; and then,
A blood-red orange, sets again.

Before the stars have left the skies,
At morning in the dark I rise;
And shivering in my nakedness,
By the cold candle, bathe and dress.

Close by the jolly fire I sit
To warm my frozen bones a bit;
Or with a reindeer-sled, explore
The colder countries round the door.

When to go out, my nurse doth wrap
Me in my comforter and cap:
The cold wind burns my face, and blows
Its frosty pepper up my nose.

Black are my steps on silver sod;
Thick blows my frosty breath abroad;
And trees and house, and hill and lake,
Are frosted like a wedding-cake.

Robert Louis Stevenson, 1850-1894

A FROSTY MORNING

O N a frosty morning with a little February sun, Clifford and Connie went for a walk across the park to the wood. That is Clifford chuffed in his motor-chair, and Connie walked beside him.

The hard air was still sulphurous, but they were both used to it. Round the near horizon went the haze, opalescent with frost and smoke, and on the top lay the small blue sky; so that it was like being inside an enclosure, always inside. Life always a dream or a frenzy, inside an enclosure.

The sheep coughed in the rough, sere grass of the park where frost lay bluish in the sockets of the tufts. Across the park ran a path to the wood-gate, a fine ribbon of pink. Clifford had had it newly gravelled with sifted gravel from the pit-bank. When the rock and refuse of the underworld had burned and given off its sulphur, it turned bright pink, shrimp-coloured on dry days, darker, crab-coloured on wet. Now it was pale shrimp-colour, with a bluish-white hoar of frost. It always pleased Connie, this underfoot of sifted, bright pink. It's an ill wind that brings nobody good.

Clifford steered cautiously down the slope of the knoll from the hall, and Connie kept her hand on the chair. In front lay the wood, the hazel thicket nearest, the purplish density of oaks beyond. From the wood's edge rabbits bobbed and nibbled. Rooks suddenly rose in a black train, and went trailing off over the little sky.

Connie opened the wood-gate, and Clifford puffed slowly through into the broad riding that ran up an incline between the clean-whipped thickets of the hazel. The wood was a remnant of the great forest where Robin Hood hunted, and this riding was an old, old thoroughfare coming across country. But now, of course, it was only a riding through the private wood. The road from Mansfield swerved round to the north.

From *Lady Chatterley's Lover* by D. H. Lawrence, 1885-1930

A SHORT TRIP HOME

Joe Jelke came in, red-faced from the cold, his white silk muffler gleaming at the neck of his fur coat. He was a senior at New Haven, I was a sophomore. He was prominent, a member of Scroll and Keys, and, in my eyes, very distinguished and handsome.

'Isn't Ellen coming?'

'I don't know,' I answered discreetly. 'She was all ready.'

'Ellen!' he called. 'Ellen!'

He had left the front door open behind him and a great cloud of frosty air rolled in from outside. He went half-way up the stairs – he was a familiar in the house – and called again, till Mrs Baker came to the banister and said that Ellen was below. Then the maid, a little excited, appeared in the dining-room door.

'Mr Jelke,' she called in a low voice.

Joe's face fell as he turned towards her, sensing bad news.

'Miss Ellen says for you to go to the party. She'll come later.'

'What's the matter?'

'She can't come now. She'll come later.'

He hesitated, confused. It was the last big dance of vacation, and he was mad about Ellen. He had tried to give her a ring for

Christmas, and failing that, got her to accept a gold mesh bag that must have cost two hundred dollars. He wasn't the only one – there were three or four in the same wild condition, and all in the ten days she'd been home – but his chance came first, for he was rich and gracious and at that moment the 'desirable' boy of St Paul. To me it seemed impossible that she could prefer another, but the rumour was she'd described Joe as much too perfect. I suppose he lacked mystery for her, and when a man is up against that with a young girl who isn't thinking of the practical side of marriage yet – well—.

F. Scott Fitzgerald, 1896-1940

THE EVE OF ST. AGNES

ST. AGNES' Eve – Ah, bitter chill it was!
The owl, for all his feathers, was a-cold;
The hare limp'd trembling through the frozen grass,
And silent was the flock in woolly fold:
Numb were the Beadsman's fingers, while he told
His rosary, and while his frosted breath,
Like pious incense from a censer old,
Seem'd taking flight for heaven, without a death,
Past the sweet Virgin's picture, while his prayer he saith.

His prayer he saith, this patient, holy man;
Then takes his lamp, and riseth from his knees,
And back returneth, meagre, barefoot, wan,
Along the chapel aisle by slow degrees:
The sculptur'd dead, on each side, seem to freeze,
Emprison'd in black purgatorial rails:
Knights, ladies, praying in dumb orat'ries,
He passeth by: and his weak spirit fails
To think how they may ache in icy hoods and mails.

Northward he turneth through a little door,
And scarce three steps, ere Music's golden tongue
Flatter'd to tears this aged man and poor;
But no – already had his deathbell rung:
The joys of all his life were said and sung:
His was harsh penance on St. Agnes' Eve:
Another way he went, and soon among
Rough ashes he sat for his soul's reprieve,
And all night kept awake, for sinners' sake to grieve.

John Keats, 1795-1821

SONNET

How like a Winter hath my absence been
From thee, the pleasure of the fleeting year!
What freezings have I felt, what dark days seen,
What old December's bareness everywhere!
And yet this time removed was summer's time;
The teeming Autumn, big with rich increase,
Bearing the wanton burden of the prime
Like widow'd wombs after their Lord's decease:
Yet this abundant issue seem'd to me
But hope of orphans and unfather'd fruit;
For Summer and his pleasures wait on thee,
And, thou away, the very birds are mute:
Or if they sing, 'tis with so dull a cheer
That leaves look pale, dreading the Winter's near.

William Shakespeare, 1564-1616

FROM THE WINDOW

THE western windows of Olive's drawing-room, looking over the water, took in the red sunsets of winter; the long, low bridge that crawled, on its staggering posts, across the Charles; the casual patches of ice and snow; the desolate suburban horizons, peeled and made bald by the rigour of the season; the general hard, cold void of the prospect; the extrusion, at Charlestown, at Cambridge, of a few chimneys and steeples, straight, sordid tubes of factories and engine-shops, or spare, heavenward finger of the New England meeting-house. There was something inexorable in the poverty of the scene, shameful in the meanness of its details, which gave a collective impression of boards and tin and frozen earth, sheds and rotting piles. . . .

Verena thought such a view lovely, and she was by no means without excuse when, as the afternoon closed, the ugly picture was tinted with a clear, cold rosiness. The air, in its windless chill, seemed to tinkle like a crystal, the faintest gradations of tone were perceptible in the sky, the west became deep and delicate, everything grew doubly distinct before taking on the dimness of evening. There were pink flushes on snow, 'tender' reflections in patches of stiffened marsh, sounds of car-bells, no longer vulgar, but almost silvery, on the long bridge, lonely outlines of distant dusky undulations against the fading glow. These agreeable effects used to light up that end of the drawing-room, and Olive often sat at the window with her companion before it was time for the lamp. They admired the sunsets, they rejoiced in the ruddy spots projected upon the parlour-wall, they followed the darkening perspective in fanciful excursions. They watched the stellar points come out at last in a colder heaven, and then, shuddering a little, arm in arm, they turned away, with a sense that the winter night was even more cruel than the tyranny of men – turned back to drawn curtains and brighter fire and a glittering tea-tray and more and more talk about the long martydom of women, a subject as to which Olive was inexhaustable and really most interesting.

From *The Bostonians* by Henry James, 1843-1916

A COLD CHRISTENING

Septuagesima Sunday, St. Valentine's Eve

PREACHED at Clyro in the morning (Matthew xiv, 30). Very few people in Church, the weather fearful, violent deadly E. wind and the hardest frost we have had yet. Went to Bettws in the afternoon wrapped in two waistcoats, two coats, a muffler and a mackintosh, and was not at all too warm. Heard the Chapel bell pealing strongly for the second time since I have been here and when I got to the Chapel my beard moustaches and whiskers were so stiff with ice that I could hardly open my mouth and my beard was frozen on to my mackintosh. There was a large christening party from Llwyn Gwilym. The baby was baptized in ice which was broken and swimming about in the Font.

From *The Diary of the Reverend Frances Kilvert*, 1870

DANCING WITH THE FEZZIWIGS

Iɴ came a fiddler with a music-book, and went up to the lofty
desk, and made an orchestra of it, and tuned like fifty
stomach-aches. In came Mrs. Fezziwig, one vast substantial smile.
In came the three Miss Fezziwigs, beaming and lovable. In came
the six young followers whose hearts they broke. In came all the
young men and women employed in the business. In came the

housemaid, with her cousin, the baker. In came the cook, with her brother's particular friend, the milkman. In came the boy from over the way, who was suspected of not having board enough from his master; trying to hide himself behind the girl from next door but one, who was proved to have had her ears pulled by her Mistress. In they all came, one after another; some shyly, some boldly, some gracefully, some awkwardly, some pushing, some pulling; in they all came, anyhow and everyhow. Away they all went, twenty couple at once, hands half round and back again the other way, down the middle and up again; round and round in various stages of affectionate grouping; old top couple always turning up in the wrong place; new top couple starting off again, as soon as they got there; all top couples at last, and not a bottom one to help them. When this result was brought about, old Fezziwig, clapping his hands to stop the dance, cried out, 'Well done!' and the fiddler plunged his hot face into a pot of porter, especially provided for that purpose. But scorning rest upon his reappearance, he instantly began again, though there were no dancers yet, as if the other fiddler had been carried home, exhausted, on a shutter; and he were a bran-new man resolved to beat him out of sight, or perish.

There were more dances, and there were forfeits, and more dances, and there was cake, and there was negus, and there was a great piece of Cold Roast, and there was a great piece of Cold, Boiled, and there were mince pies, and plenty of beer. But the great effect of the evening came after the Roast and Boiled, when the fiddler (an artful dog, mind! The sort of man who knew his business better than you or I could have told it him!) struck up 'Sir Roger de Coverley.' Then old Fezziwig stood out to dance with Mrs. Fezziwig. Top couple, too; with a good stiff piece of work cut out for them; three or four and twenty pair of partners; people who were not to be trifled with; people who *would* dance, and had no notion of walking.

From *A Christmas Carol* by Charles Dickens, 1812-1870

SNOW

THERE is a line of poetry so familiar to me that I well might inadvertently think it mine, and be blamed for passing off as my own something not of my making; a line mixed so closely with the working of my mind that it comes back to me every winter whenever the transforming snowfall alters the ordinary aspect of fields and woods. I am not sure where it comes from, but I fancy it is by Ralph Waldo Emerson, whose poetical works I do not happen to possess, and it runs.

The frolic architecture of the snow.

I am not sure either whether it is good poetry or not – a little precious, perhaps, a little whimsical – but it does convey something to me of the quality fresh snow gives to the landscape, something of the black-and-whiteness, the emphasized design of boundaries, the darkness of water, the toss of trees. Frolic. Yes, it has an altering touch; nothing else is like it. Of course, to be beautiful, snow must be thick and fresh; the patchy days of thaw are Nature at her ugliest, when it is better to avert the eyes until everything is green and brown again.

The recent show was preceded by three days of something even more beautiful, something which the foot of man does not smirch, nor the ruts of his waggon wheels impair. The hoar frost is inviolable. Each twig and blade sparkled separately, as the big red sun came slowly overlaying the whiteness with a tinge of pink. The world was so crisp, you could almost hear it crackle. On every pane of the windows the frost had drawn patterns as exquisite as the veining of transparent leaves, no two alike, in a very low relief which one traced with the tip of a finger sending correspondent filaments of cold up the veining of one's arm. A thing to be noted during the days of hoar frost was the peculiar brilliant green of moss in woodland paths. It came through the whiteness with an almost vicious viridescence.

From *Country Notes in Wartime* by Vita Sackville-West, 1892-1962

THE CHRISTMAS DANCE

IT was a lively scene, for soon the spirit of the social season took
possession of everyone, and Christmas merriment made all
faces shine, hearts happy, and heels light. The musicians fiddled,
tooted, and banged as if they enjoyed it; everybody danced who
could, and those who couldn't admired their neighbours with
uncommon warmth. The air was dark with Davises, and many
Joneses gambolled like a flock of young giraffes. The golden
secretary darted through the room like a meteor, with a dashing
Frenchwoman who carpeted the floor with her pink satin train.
The Serene Teuton found the supper-table, and was happy, eating
steadily through the bill of fare, and dismaying the garçons by the

ravages he committed. But the Emperor's friend covered himself with glory, for he danced *everything*, whether he knew it or not, and introduced impromptu pirouettes when the figures bewildered him. The boyish abandon of that stout man was charming to behold; for, though he 'carried weight', he danced like an india-rubber ball. He ran, he flew, he pranced; his face glowed, his bald head shone, his coat tails waved wildly, his pumps actually twinkled in the air, and when the music stopped, he wiped the drops from his brow, and beamed upon his fellow-men like a French Pickwick without glasses.

Amy and her Pole distinguished themselves by equal enthusiasm, but more graceful agility; and Laurie found himself involuntarily keeping time to the rhythmic rise and fall of the white slippers, as they flew by, as indefatigably as if winged. When little Vladimir finally relinquished her, with assurances that he was 'desolated to leave so early', she was ready to rest, and see how her recreant knight had borne his punishment. It had been successful; for, at three-and-twenty, blighted affections find a balm in friendly society, and young nerves will thrill, young blood dance, and healthy young spirits rise, when subjected to the enchantment of beauty, light, music, and motion. Laurie had a waked-up look as he rose to give her his seat; and when he hurried away to bring her some supper, she said to herself with a satisfied smile;

'Ah, I thought that would do him good!'

'You look like Balzac's "Femme peinte par elle-même",' he said, as he fanned her with one hand, and held her coffee-cup in the other.

'My rouge won't come off;' and Amy rubbed her brilliant cheek, and showed him her white glove, with a sober simplicity that made him laugh outright.

'What do you call this stuff?' he asked, touching a fold of her dress that had blown over his knee.

'Illusion.'

From *Good Wives* by Louisa M. Alcott, 1832-1888

SONG

WHEN icicles hang by the wall,
And Dick the shepherd blows his nail.
And Tom bears logs into the hall,
And milk comes frozen home in pail,
When blood is nipp'd and ways be foul,
Then nightly sings the staring owl,
To-whit!
To-who! – a merry note,
While greasy Joan doth keel the pot.

When all aloud the wind doth blow,
And coughing drowns the parson's saw,
And birds sit brooding in the snow,
And Marian's nose looks red and raw,
When roasted crabs hiss in the bowl,
Then nightly sings the staring owl,
To-whit!
To-who! – a merry note,
While greasy Joan doth keel the pot.

William Shakespeare, 1564-1616

WINTER IN THE KITCHEN

WINTER was no more typical of our valley than summer, it was not even summer's opposite; it was merely that other place. And somehow one never remembered the journey towards it; one arrived, and winter was here. The day came suddenly when all details were different and the village had to be rediscovered. One's nose went dead so that it hurt to breathe, and there were jigsaws of frost on the window. The light filled the house with a green polar glow; while outside – in the invisible world – there was a strange hard silence, or a metallic creaking, a faint throbbing of twigs and wires.

The kitchen that morning would be full of steam, billowing from kettles and pots. The outside pump was frozen again, making a sound like broken crockery, so that the girls tore icicles from the eaves for water and we drank boiled ice in our tea.

'It's wicked,' said Mother. 'The poor, poor birds.' And she flapped her arms with vigour.

She and the girls were wrapped in all they had, coats and scarves and mittens; some had the shivers and some drops on their noses, while poor little Phyllis sat rocking in a chair holding her chilblains like a handful of bees.

There was an iron-shod clatter down the garden path and the milkman pushed open the door. The milk in his pail was frozen solid. He had to break off lumps with a hammer.

'It's murder out,' the milkman said. 'Crows worryin' the sheep. Swans froze in the lake. An' tits droppin' dead in mid air . . .' He drank his tea while his eyebrows melted, slapped Dorothy's bottom, and left.

From *Cider with Rosie* by Laurie Lee, 1914-

PICTURE-BOOKS
IN WINTER

SUMMER fading, winter comes –
Frosty mornings, tingling thumbs,
Window robins, winter rooks,
And the picture story-books.

Water now is turned to stone
Nurse and I can walk upon;
Still we find the flowing brooks
In the picture story-books.

All the pretty things put by,
Wait upon the children's eye,
Sheep and shepherds, trees and crooks,
In the picture story-books.

We may see how all things are,
Seas and cities, near and far,
And the flying fairies' looks,
In the picture story-books.

How am I to sing your praise,
Happy chimney-corner days,
Sitting safe in nursery nooks,
Reading picture story-books?

Robert Louis Stevenson, 1850-1894

BLOW, BLOW,
THOU WINTER WIND

BLOW, blow, thou winter wind,
Thou art not so unkind
As man's ingratitude;
Thy tooth is not so keen,
Because thou art not seen,
Although thy breath be rude.
Heigh ho! sing, heigh ho! unto the green holly:
Most friendship is feigning, most loving mere folly;
Then heigh ho, the holly!
This life is most jolly.

Freeze, freeze, thou bitter sky,
That dost not bite so nigh
As benefits forgot:
Though thou the waters warp,
Thy sting is not so sharp
As friend remember'd not.
Heigh ho! sing, heigh ho! unto the green holly:
Most friendship is feigning, most loving mere folly;
Then heigh ho, the holly!
This life is most jolly.

William Shakespeare, 1564-1616

Neutral Tones

We stood by a pond that winter day,
And the sun was white, as though chidden of God,
And a few leaves lay on the starving sod;
 – They had fallen from an ash, and were gray.

Your eyes on me were as eyes that rove
Over tedious riddles of years ago;
And some words played between us to and fro'
On which lost the more by our love.

The smile on your mouth was the deadest thing
Alive enough to have strength to die;
And a grin of bitterness swept thereby
Like an ominous bird a-wing . . .

Since then, keen lessons that love deceives,
And wrings with wrong, have shaped to me
Your face, and the God-curst sun, and a tree,
And a pond edged with grayish leaves.

Thomas Hardy, 1840-1928

THE CHRISTMAS HOLIDAYS

FINE old Christmas, with the snowy hair and ruddy face, had done his duty that year in the noblest fashion, and had set off his rich gifts of warmth and colour with all the heightening contrast of frost and snow. And yet this Christmas day, in spite of Tom's fresh delight in home, was not, he thought, somehow or other, quite so happy as it had always been before. The red berries were just as abundant on the holly, and he and Maggie had dressed all the windows and mantelpieces and picture-frames on Christmas Eve with as much taste as ever, wedding the thick-set scarlet clusters with branches of the black-berried ivy. There had been singing under the windows after midnight – supernatural singing, Maggie always felt, in spite of Tom's contemptuous insistence that the singers were old Patch, the parish clerk, and the rest of the church choir: she trembled with awe when their carolling broke in upon her dreams, and the image of men in fustian clothes was always thrust away by the vision of angels resting on the parted cloud. But the midnight chant had helped as usual to lift the morning above the level of common days; and then there was the smell of hot toast and ale from the kitchen at the breakfast hour; the favourite anthem, the green boughs and the short sermon, gave the appropriate festal character to the church-going; and aunt and uncle Moss, with all their seven children, were looking like so many reflectors of the bright parlour fire, when the church-goers came back, stamping the snow from their feet. The plum-pudding was of the same handsome roundness as ever, and came in with the symbolic blue flames around it, as if it had been heroically snatched from the nether fires into which it had been thrown by dyspeptic Puritans; the dessert was as splendid as ever, with its golden oranges; brown nuts, and the crystalline light and dark of apple jelly and damson cheese: in all these things Christmas was as it had always been since Tom could remember; it was only distinguished, if by anything, by superior sliding and snowballs.

From *The Mill on the Floss* by George Eliot, 1819-1880

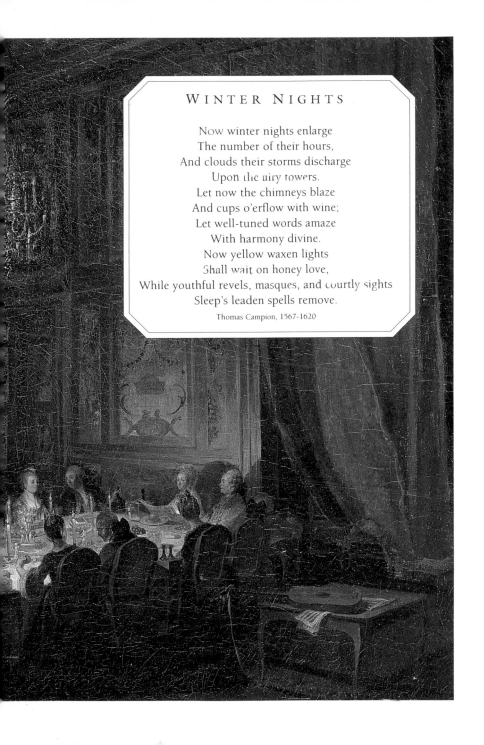

WINTER NIGHTS

Now winter nights enlarge
The number of their hours,
And clouds their storms discharge
Upon the airy towers.
Let now the chimneys blaze
And cups o'erflow with wine;
Let well-tuned words amaze
With harmony divine.
Now yellow waxen lights
Shall wait on honey love,
While youthful revels, masques, and courtly sights
Sleep's leaden spells remove.

Thomas Campion, 1567-1620

GATHERING HOLLY

As for the Log-house, it is full. We have cut down several trees, and huge Yule logs lie in heaps, ready for the hall fire. We shall want them before the winter is over. If Horace had to say to Thaliarchus in Italy (this is Lord Denman's version) –

> 'Dissolve the cold, while on the dogs
> With lavish hand you fling the logs,' –

surely in these northern latitudes, and in this dearth of coal, the advice is doubly seasonable. And then a log fire is so charming.

But besides the dead wood, we have just cut our fresh Christmas boughs. Up against an outhouse, I have an immense Ivy, almost as large as one you see growing up some old castle: it spreads along the wall, covering it all over on both sides; then it climbs up a second wall at right angles to the first, and throws its trailing branches down to the very ground; and now they are one mass of blossom.

It is from this ivy that we gather our best Christmas greenery; but there are also cuttings from the Box, Yew, and Holly; – and one variegated Holly has been beautiful, for its mottled leaves have in some sprays become of a perfectly clear and creamy white – the colour of fine old ivory. Mistletoe does not grow with us, and we have to buy it in the market of our town.

From *A Year in a Lancashire Garden* by Henry A. Bright

WINTER

Autumn crept along that special year well into December. We had sweet peas and dahlias still in bloom, as well as a quantity of outdoor chrysanthemums. The Christmas roses were put under a species of thatched roof to protect them from any frost that might come before the buds had expanded widely enough to put the handlights over them, and the *Gloire de Dijon* roses over the front of the house were well out in flower. Indeed, there are few years that I have not gathered roses somewhere in December. Even in our last year in London I picked pale-red roses off a rambler the day before Christmas, and I fancy the people who continually write to the papers wonderful accounts of the blossoms they have discovered at unexpected seasons, must only at that moment have had their eyes open. No winter I ever passed in Dorsetshire, and I spent, I think, sixteen there altogether, went by without roses, winter-heliotrope, violets, primroses and poly-anthus, to say nothing of veronica, which, if judiciously chosen, can be obtained to bloom at almost every season in the year.

From *Leaves from a Garden* by Miss Parton, c1910

GWENDOLEN

GWENDOLEN was already mounted and riding down the avenue when Rex appeared at the gate. She provided herself against disappontment in case he didn't appear in time by having the groom ready behind her she would not have waited beyond a reasonable time. But now the groom was dismissed, and the two rode away in delightful freedom. Gwendolen was in her highest spirits, and Rex thought that she had never looked so lovely before; her figure, her long white throat, and the curves of her cheek and chin were always set off to perfection by the compact simplicity of her riding dress. He could not conceive a more perfect girl; and to a youthful lover like Rex it seems that the fundamental identity of the good, the true and the beautiful, is already extant and manifest in the subject of his love. Most observers would have held it more than equally accountable that a girl should have like impressions about Rex, for in his handsome face there was nothing corresponding to the undefinable stinging quality – that were a trace of demon ancestry – which made some beholders hesitate in their admiration of Gwendolen.

It was an exquisite January morning in which there was a threat of rain, but a grey sky making the calmest of ground for the charms of a mild winter scene: – the grassy borders of the lanes, the hedgerows sprinkled with red berries and haunted with low twitterings, the purple bareness of the elms, the rich brown of the furrows.

From *Daniel Deronda* by George Eliot, 1819-1880

AT THE OPERA

O N a January evening of the early seventies, Christine Nilsson was singing in *Faust* at the Academy of Music in New York. Though there was already talk of the erection; in remote metropolitan distances 'above the Forties', of a new Opera House which should compete in costliness and splendour with those of the great European capitals, the world of fashion was still content to reassemble every winter in the shabby red and gold boxes of the sociable old Academy. Conservatives cherished it for being small and inconvenient, and thus keeping out the 'new people' whom New York was beginning to dread and yet be drawn to; and the sentimental clung to it for its historic associations, and the musical for its excellent acoustics, always so problematic a quality in halls built for the hearing of music.

It was Madame Nilsson's first appearance that winter, and what the daily press had already learned to describe as 'an exceptionally brilliant audience' had gathered to hear her, transported through the slippery, snowy streets in private broughams, in the spacious family landau, or in the humbler but more convenient 'Brown *coupé*'. To come to the Opera in a Brown *coupé*, was almost as honourable a way of arriving as in one's own carriage; and departure by the same means had the immense advantage of enabling one (with a playful allusion to democratic principles) to scramble into the first Brown conveyance in the line, instead of waiting till the cold-and-gin-congested nose of one's own coachman gleamed under the portico of the Acadamy. It was one of the great livery-stableman's most masterly intuitions to have discovered that Americans want to get away from amusement even more quickly than they want to get to it.

From *The Age of Innocence* by Edith Wharton, 1862-1937

WINTER FANCIES

WINTER without
And warmth within;
The winds may shout
And the storm begin;
The snows may pack
At the window-pane,
And the skies grow black,
And the sun remain
Hidden away
The livelong day –
But here – in here is the warmth of May!

Swoop your spitefullest
Up the flue,
Wild Winds – do!
What in the world do I care for you?

O delightfullest
Weather of all,
Howl and squall,
And shake the trees till the last leaves fall!

James Whitcomb Riley, 1849-1916

KITTY AND LEVIN

A T four o'clock that afternoon Levin, conscious that his heart was beating rapidly, got out of the hired sledge at the Zoological Gardens and went down the path leading to the ice-hills and skating lake, sure of finding Kitty there, for he had noticed the Shcherbatskys' carriage at the entrance.

It was a clear frosty day. Carriages, private sledges, sledges for hire, and mounted police stood at the entrance. Well-dressed people, their hats shining in the sunlight, crowded at the gates and thronged the clean-swept paths between little houses built with carved eaves in Russian style. The bushy birch trees in the Garden with all their branches weighed down by snow seemed attired in new festive garments. He walked along the path leading to the skating lake, and kept repeating to himself: 'I must not be excited, I must be quiet! . . . What are you doing? What's the matter? Be quiet, stupid!' he said to his heart. But the more he tried to be calm, the more laboured grew his breath. He met an acquaintance who called to him, but Levin did not even notice who it was. He approached the ice-hills and heard the clanking of the chains by which the sledges were being pulled up, their clatter as they descended the hills, and the sound of merry voices. A few more steps brought him to the skating lake, and among all the skaters he at once recognize her.

On that day of the week and at that hour, people belonging to the same set and acquainted with one another, met on the ice. Among them were masters of the art of skating showing off their skill, and beginners with timid and awkward movements holding on to the backs of chairs fitted with runners; boys, and old men skating for hygienic reasons; and they all seemed to Levin to be fortune's favourites because they were here near her. Yet skaters appeared quite calmly to gain on her, to catch her up, and even to speak to her, and quite independently of her to amuse themselves enjoying the excellent ice and the fine weather.

Nicholas Shcherbatsky, Kitty's cousin, in a short jacket, tight trousers, with skates on his feet, was sitting on a bench, and seeing Levin, called out to him.

'Hullo you Russian champion skater! When did you come? The ice is splendid – put on your skates!'

'I haven't any skates,' answered Levin, wondering at such boldness and freedom of manner in her presence, and not losing sight of her for a moment although not looking at her. He felt the sun approaching him. She was turning a corner, her little feet, shod in high boots, kept close together, and she was skating timidly toward him. A little boy dressed in a Russian costume, violently swinging his arms and stooping very low, was overtaking her.

She was not very firm on her feet. Having drawn her hands from the muff that hung by a cord from her neck, she held them out and looking at Levin, whom she had recognized, she smiled at him and at her fears. Having turned the corner, she pushed off with an elastic little foot, glided straight up to Shcherbatsky, and catching hold of him wth her hand, nodded smilingly to Levin. She was more beautiful than he had imagined her.

From *Anna Karenina* by Leo Tolstoy, 1828-1910

LONDON SNOW

WHEN men were all asleep the snow came flying,
In large white flakes falling on the city brown,
Stealthily and perpetually settling and loosely lying,
Hushing the latest traffic of the drowsy town;
Deadening, muffling, stifling its murmurs failing;
Lazily and incessantly floating down and down:
Silently sifting and veiling road, roof and railing;
Hiding difference, making unevenness even,
Into angles and crevices softly drifting and sailing.
All night it fell, and when full inches seven
It lay in the depth of its uncompacted lightness,
The clouds blew off from a high and frosty heaven;
And all woke earlier for the unaccustomed brightness
Of the winter dawning, the strange unheavenly glare:
The eye marvelled – marvelled at the dazzling whiteness;
The ear hearkened to the stillness of the solemn air;
No sound of wheel rumbling nor of foot falling,
And the busy morning cries came thin and spare.
Then boys I heard, as they went to school, calling,
They gathered up the crystal manna to freeze
Their tongues with tasting, their hands with snowballing;

Or rioted in a drift, plunging up to the knees;
Or peering up from under the white-mossed wonder,
'O look at the trees!' they cried, 'O look at the trees!'

Robert Bridges, 1844-1930

WAITING

OCTOBER, November, December passed away. One afternoon in January, Mrs Fairfax had begged a holiday for Adèle, because she had a cold; and, as Adèle seconded the request with an ardour that minded me how precious occasional holidays had been to me in my own childhood, I accorded it, deeming that I did well in showing plausibility on that point. It was a fine, calm day, though very cold; I was tired of sitting still in the library, through a whole long morning: Mrs Fairfax had just written a letter which was waiting to be posted, so I put on my bonnet and cloak and volunteered to carry it to Hay; the distance, two miles, would be a pleasant winter afternoon walk. Having seen Adèle comfortably seated in her little chair by Mrs Fairfax's parlour fireside, and given her her best wax doll (which I usually kept enveloped in silver paper in a drawer) to play with, and a story-book for change of amusement; and having replied to her 'Revenez bien tôt, ma bonne amie, ma chère Mdlle Jeannette,' with a kiss, I set off.

The ground was hard, the air was still, my road was lonely. I walked fast till I got warm, and then I walked slowly to enjoy and analyse the species of pleasure brooding for me in the hour and situation. It was three o'clock; the church bell tolled as I passed under the belfry; the charm of the hour lay in its approaching dimness, in the low-gliding and pale-beaming sun. I was a mile from Thornfield; the lane noted for wild roses in summer, for nuts and blackberries in autumn, and even now possessing a few coral treasures in hips and haws, but whose best winter delight lay in its utter solitude and fearless repose. If a breath of air stirred, it made no sound here; for there was not a holly, not an evergreen to rustle, and the stripped hawthorn and hazel bushes were as still as the white worn stones which causewayed the middle of the path. Fat and wide, on each side, there were only fields, where no cattle now browsed; and the little brown birds which stirred occasionally in the hedge, looked like single russet leaves that had forgotten to drop.

This lane inclined uphill all the way to Hay; having reached the middle, I sat down on a stile which led thence into a field. Gathering my mantle about me, and sheltering my hands in my muff, I did not feel the cold, though it froze keenly; as was attested by a sheet of ice covering the causeway, where a little brooklet, now congealed, had overflowed after a rapid thaw some days since. From my seat I could look down on Thornfield: the gray and battlemented hall was the principal object in the vale below me; its woods and dark rookery rose against the west. I lingered till the sun went down amongst the trees, and sank crimson and clear behind them.

From *Jane Eyre* by Charlotte Brontë, 1816-1855

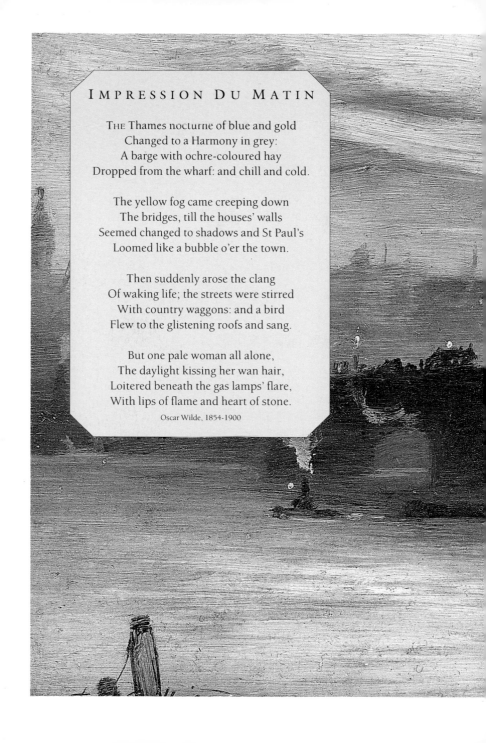

IMPRESSION DU MATIN

THE Thames nocturne of blue and gold
Changed to a Harmony in grey:
A barge with ochre-coloured hay
Dropped from the wharf: and chill and cold.

The yellow fog came creeping down
The bridges, till the houses' walls
Seemed changed to shadows and St Paul's
Loomed like a bubble o'er the town.

Then suddenly arose the clang
Of waking life; the streets were stirred
With country waggons: and a bird
Flew to the glistening roofs and sang.

But one pale woman all alone,
The daylight kissing her wan hair,
Loitered beneath the gas lamps' flare,
With lips of flame and heart of stone.

Oscar Wilde, 1854-1900

A REGENCY REVEL

IMMEDIATELY surrounding Mrs. Musgrove were the little Harvilles, whom she was sedulously guarding from the tyranny of the two children from the Cottage, expressly arrived to amuse them. On one side was a table, occupied by some chattering girls, cutting up silk and gold paper; and on the other were tressels and trays, bending under the weight of brawn and cold pies, where riotous boys were holding high revel; the whole completed by a roaring Christmas fire, which seemed determined to be heard, in spite of all the noise of the others; Charles and Mary also came in, of course, during their visit; and Mr. Musgrove made a point of paying his respects to Lady Russell, and sat down close to her for ten minutes, talking with a very raised voice, but, from the clamour of the children on his knees, generally in vain. It was a fine family-piece.

Anne, judging from her own temperament, would have deemed such a domestic hurricane a bad restorative of the nerves, which Louisa's illness must have so greatly shaken; but Mrs. Musgrove, who got Anne near her on purpose to thank her most cordially, again and again, for all her attentions to them, concluded a short recapitulation of what she had suffered herself, by observing, with a happy glance round the room, that after all she had gone through, nothing was so likely to do her good as a little quiet cheerfulness at home.

From *Persuasion* by Jane Austen, 1775-1817

STOPPING BY WOODS
ON A SNOWY EVENING

WHOSE woods these are I think I know.
His house is in the village, though;
He will not see me stopping here
To watch his woods fill up with snow.

My little horse must think it queer
To stop without a farmhouse near
Between the woods and frozen lake
The darkest evening of the year.

He gives his harness bells a shake
To ask if there is some mistake.
The only other sound's the sweep
Of easy wind and downy flake.

The woods are lovely, dark, and deep,
But I have promises to keep,
And miles to go before I sleep,
And miles to go before I sleep.

Robert Frost, 1874-1963

ACKNOWLEDGEMENTS

Bridgeman Art Library:
p3 *Winter Scene and Figures Skating*: Esaias I Van de Velde/Harold Samuel Collection, Corporation of London; p7 *The Fern Gatherer*: C S Lidderdale/Phillips International Fine Art Auctioneers; p11 *Portrait of Mrs Kathleen Newton*: James Jacques Tissot/ Private Collection; p12 *Man in a Fur Coat*: Robert Oswald Moser/Christopher Wood Gallery, London; p15 *Ode to Music*: John Melhuish Strudwick/Roy Miles Fine Paintings, London; p21 *The Christening* (detail): Edward Bird/Wolverhampton Art Gallery; p22 *Mr Fezziwig's Ball*: John Leech/V&A; p25 *The Trianon Under Snow*: Henri Eugene Augustin Le Sidaner/Private Collection; p26 *The Waltz*: Joseph Marius Avy/Whitford & Hughes, London; p29 *February, Les Tres Riches Heures du Duc de Berry*/V&A; p30 *Home*: Carlton Alfred Smith/Christie's, London; p37 *Winter Days*: George Henry Boughton/Fine Art Society, London; p38 *Snowballing*: Cornelius Kimmel/Gavin Graham Gallery, London; p39 *Advertisement for Christmas Hampers*/ Private Collection; p40/41 *Dinner at the Temple of Prince of Conti*: Michel Barthelemy Olivier/Chateau de Versailles, France; p43 *Christmas Roses*: Willem van Leen/Gavin Graham Gallery, London; p44 *Mlle Croizette*: Charles Emile Auguste Carolus-Duran/ Musée Des Beaux Arts, Touring; p46 *Franz Schubert at the Piano*: Gustav Klimt/ Archiv Für Kunst und Geschichte, Berlin; p48 *My Second Sermon*: Sir John Everett Millais/Guildhall Art Gallery; p55 *A Woman by a Fireside*: Marcus Stone/Agnew & Sons, London; p59 *The Clifton Assembly Rooms*: Rolinda Sharples/City of Bristol Museum & Art Gallery; p61 *A Day in Late Autumn*: E W Waite/Private Collection; p63 *The Mistletoe Gatherer*: Sir John Everett Millais/Private Collection.

David Messum Galleries, London & Beaconsfield:
p13 *The Evening Shawl*: Archibald Barnes; p18 *The Goldfish Bowl*: Wilfred de Glehn; p33 *Fairy Tales*: George Harcourt.

Fine Art Photographic Archive:
p9 *Carriage to a Ball*: William Bromley; p17 *Madame Se Chauffe*: John Callcott Horsley; p20 *New Year's Eve*: William Henry Boot; p42 *Flowers of Shakespeare*: Anon; p45 *Redwing During Frost*: Archibald Thorburn; p47 *Paris*: Louis Besson; p56/57 *St Paul's from the River*: George Hyde Pownall.

Manya Igel Fine Arts/The Medici Society: p5 *Frozen Out*: George Dunlop Leslie.

National Gallery:
p35 *A Winter Scene with Skaters near a Castle*: Henrick Avercamp.

Richard Hagen Fine Paintings, Worcestershire:
p50 *The Skater* (detail): Edward John Gregory.

Royal Academy of Arts: p52 *Green Park*: Robert Buhler.

Cover: *The Mistletoe Gatherer*: Sir John Everett Millais/Private Collection/ The Bridgeman Art Library.

THE WINTER GARDEN

The Winter Garden which scents the endpapers of this book was created for that season of the year when the garden is no longer producing fragrant blossoms which we can cut and bring indoors. This scent for the Christmas season is inspired by the spicy food we eat and the hot toddies we drink. It contains cloves and cinnamon and evokes the days when the wassail bowl was enjoyed in front of a roaring fire whilst the snow lay on the ground outside.

The pot-pourri contains chillies, star aniseed from Asia, cedar wings, the small cassurina cone, and blue mallow and hibiscus dried from an English garden.

Published in the United States by Harmony Books,
a division of Crown Publishers, Inc.,
201 East 50th Street, New York, New York 10022

First published in Great Britain in 1992 by Pavilion Books Limited

Harmony and Colophon are trademarks of Crown Publishers, Inc.

Manufactured in Singapore by Imago

ISBN 0-517-58940-0

First American Edition

10 9 8 7 6 5 4 3 2 1

If you would like more information on
Penhaligon's The Winter Garden, with which this book is scented,
or any other of the Penhaligon gifts or products,
please telephone London 011-44-81-880-2050, or write to:
PENHALIGON'S
41 Wellington Street, Covent Garden, London WC2